Springtime

by

Jackie Reynolds

Dimpled Hippo

With love to my Mom
and to the many incredible women
I've been blessed to have had in my life...

Illustrated by: Kate Parfyreva
https://www.fiverr.com/katushkanaushko

Published by: Dimpled Hippo
Jackie Reynolds, Milan, New York 12571
Printed in the United States of America

Additional copies available by visiting:
www.BeeBeeTheClown.com/books/

Springtime

That morning the girl scooped up her teddy bear and ran to the backyard where a split rail fence stopped the meadow from growing into the garden.

"It's here! It's finally here!" she said, laughing to herself.

Overnight spring had billowed into the countryside, bringing its own circus. The wind and sunshine worked as roustabouts. They unrolled a green carpet, polished the pond into a sparkling center ring, and set up a sky blue big-top.

Purple lilacs and orange azaleas decorated the yard with giant bouquets of circus balloons.

Pink apple blossoms and leafy, green willow trees grew into big bunches of soft cotton candy.

"Presenting our tremendous circus ban[d]"
said the girl.

Woodpeckers tapped on trees.

"Let's go to the circus!" the girl sa[id]
teddy bear.

Frogs peeped in the marsh.

Geese honked in the big-top.

A red winged blackbird sang a solo by

center ring.

to the c[...]

"Ladybugs and b[...]

Birds and worms of all age[...]

Welcome to the circus!"

Her little red boots moved Left, Right, Left, and Right to the music of the circus band.

The girl said, "Such perfect music for a circus."

The circus band was an alarm clock for the back yard.
Dandelions woke up in the grass.

Daffodils yawned in their flower beds.

Forsythia stretched by the fence.

Hyacinths fixed tall hairdos and splashed on perfume.

The girl whistled her best whistle and announced, "Caterpillars and butterflies!

Squirrels and owls of all ages!
Now! The circus animal parade!"

Small, puffy poodle clouds pranced along behind the wispy tails of horses.

A herd of white elephant clouds and gray dragon clouds rock-and-rolled across the blue.

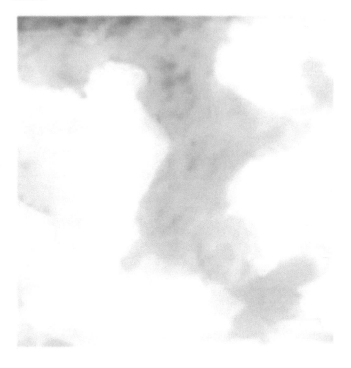

"This is the best circus parade ever!" said the girl.

Four geese flew through the parade. They
made a honking-flapping-splish-splash
landing onto center ring.

The girl laughed. "Clowns! The silly
clowns are here!" she said.

Like two keystone cops and two masked bandits the geese honked and flapped, splashed and chased each other around the water. They flew away still honking over the marsh.

The girl smiled and said, "Silly clowns!"

She climbed onto the split rail fence and called, "Circus treats! Get your circus treats right here!"

A bullfrog wearing a vest of rhinestone water droplets hopped onto a lily pad pedestal.

A mosquito cruised around the sunbeams above the water.

With the skill of a lion tamer's whip, the bullfrog's tongue tapped the mosquito on the shoulder and invited it to lunch. "Gulllumm!" said the frog as he swallowed.

A robin in an orange apron scooted across the green carpet. She was a hotdog vendor delivering a worm. As she flew to her nest hidden among the lilac circus balloons, raucous squawks of bottomless beaks sounded a sweet harmony. The robin was a gourmet chef at a circus buffet.

The girl balanced on the top rail of the fence and held her teddy bear against her jacket. She announced, "Chipmunks and pollywogs! Turtles and ducks of all ages! Now, on the high platform, Teddy the Brave!"

A flock of barn swallows watched from the cheap seats on a telephone wire.

The girl jumped down. Her boots landed in a muddy puddle with a splash.

"Ta Da!" she said.

The performance brought her audience to their wings. The birds flew away in search of a snack.

Small squadrons of gnats patrolled center ring, ready to begin another season of annoyance. Like trapeze artists without a net, the barn swallows made acrobatic swoops and death defying dives as they snatched the gnats just above the water's surface.

"Look, Teddy!" said the girl.

"The bugs bug the swallows,

and the swallows swallow the bugs!"

The wind picked up three crows. It juggled them around the meadow and dropped them into a bunch of green cotton candy. The big-top was filled with impatient dragons and heavy elephants.

A raindrop landed on the teddy bear's cheek and became a tear.

"Oh no, Teddy, rain!" cried the girl. She ran across the green carpet to the house. "We were having so much fun. Why does it rain on our circus?" she said.

Dark dragons and charcoal elephants paraded in the big-top above center ring. An elephant stepped on a dragon's tail. The dragon flashed lightning across the big top.

The girl watched through the window.

Rain stomped on the green carpet.

Rain splattered in muddy puddles.

Rain stampeded across center ring.

"Too much rain," said the girl.

Finally, gusty roustabouts swept the dragons and elephants from the big-top. Little, white poodles and small horses pranced in to finish the show.

Sunbeams mopped up the puddles and dumped fresh sparkles onto center ring. Breezes put bounces back into the big bunches of green cotton candy.

The crows laughed, "Caw, caw, caw!"

The girl ran to the backyard with her teddy bear. Performers in circus costumes were everywhere. Bumble bees with racing stripes revved their engines and zoomed around the azaleas.

Humming birds in sequined suits flitted by the hyacinths.

The gourmet chef prepared another meal for baby robins.

For the grand finale a rainbow of emeralds, rubies, and sapphires unrolled across the big top.

Silly geese slid down the rainbow and splashed into the water of center ring.

The crows laughed, "Caw, caw, caw!"

"See Teddy!" said the girl. "Both rain and rainbows are in a circus of life."

Both adults and children enjoy *Springtime*.

In addition to this kid-friendly story, the books below may be happy additions to a child's library, encouraging them to use their imagination to see the world around them in a different way.

The Picnic Circus: A Girl and Kitty Cat and *The Picnic Circus: A Boy and Puppy Dog* are created for children ages 3-7 with pictures to color in a fun story based on *Springtime*.

Young artists, ages 5-10, can create imaginative "Do It Yourself Illustrations" in a large format book (8.5"x11") with limited words. *The Circus of Life: Springtime with Bee Bee: A Book for Drawing & Coloring* has room for creative doodles and art based on a *Springtime* theme.

Made in the USA
Middletown, DE
06 August 2020

14446433R10024